KUNLEKTRA MURDER MYSTERY LOGIC PUZZLES

Enhance your mind with True Crime Puzzles

Copyright © 2023 by Kunlektra Brain Teaser

This book is for:

HOW TO SOLVE

Introducing Murder Mystery Volume 1, the official publication of Mona's Enigma, the world's most brilliant mystery solver, case files.

These memoirs of the life of a crime-fighter, in contrast to others, are riddles that you must solve rather than just stories. And all it takes to solve these situations is a keen pencil and an even keener intellect.

Let's examine Mona's Enigma's initial case to demonstrate this. The detective was positive that one of three persons had stolen the famous painting from the museum:

Alex, a skilled art forger with an uncanny ability to replicate the intricate details of renowned masterpieces, weaving a web of intrigue with each stroke of the brush as they blur the lines between authenticity and imitation.

Bella, a vigilant museum security guard, safeguards priceless artifacts with a keen eye for detail, ensuring the preservation of history against the threat of theft or vandalism.

Chris, an art collector with an affinity for the avant-garde, curates a captivating home gallery, showcasing a diverse collection that reflects a deep appreciation for creativity and cultural expression.

The thief had to know the secret code to disable the security system. The Detective also know the locations of these three suspects.

Alex was seen near the museum on the night of the theft.

Bella's alibi checks out; she was at a family gathering.

Chris has a solid alibi, as he was attending an art auction in another city.

Can you deduce who stole "Mona's Enigma"?

CLUE:

The thief had to know the secret code to disable the security system.

SOLUTION:

The thief is Alex. The key clue is that the thief had to know the secret code to disable the security system, and Alex was seen near the museum on the night of the theft.

GET STARTED WITH MODERN MYSTERIES LOGIC PUZZLE BOOK

Kunlektra Brain Teasers

1. THE POISONED COCKTAIL 

At a lavish cocktail party, Evelyn, a wealthy socialite, collapses abruptly, casting a somber shadow over the glamorous affair as the festivities turn to whispers of shock and mystery surrounding her sudden demise.

SUSPECTS

RICHARD

Her husband Richard, a wealthy businessman, becomes the center of rumors and intrigues the affluent gathering.

LILY

Her closest friend Lily struggles to deal with Evelyn's abrupt death, navigating a sea of emotions as the colorful web of their friendship unravels in the wake of the unanticipated catastrophe.

MAX

Bartender Max watches the drama of the cocktail party with a studied indifference, going from being a drink mixer to an unintentional witness to the strange thing going on.

LOCATIONS

Richard was away on a business trip and just returned that evening.

Lily and Evelyn was in Lily's cozy apartment before the party.

Max had been at the upscale lounge mixing drink for the guest of the party.

Who poisoned Evelyn's cocktail?

CLUE:
Evelyn had been receiving threatening letters recently.

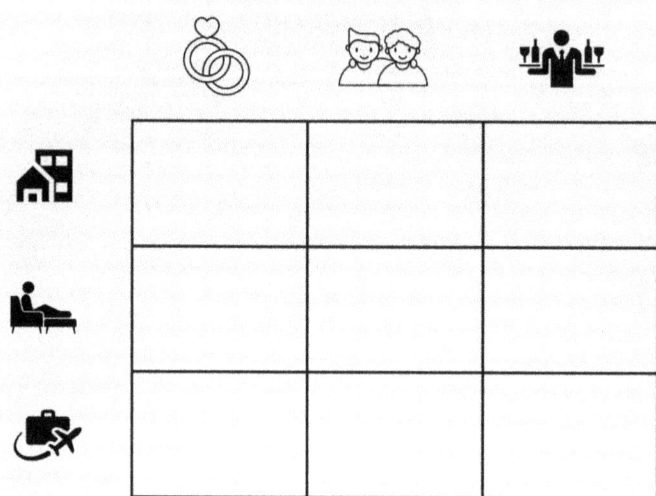

2. THE ENCHANTED ELIXIR

Renowned alchemist, Professor Alaric Alchemy, was found dead in his enchanted laboratory.
The murder weapon is a poisoned magical elixir.

SUSPECTS

EVANGELINE

His ambitious potion maker

MORTIMER

His estranged magical researcher

LOCATIONS

Evangeline was In the potion-making chamber, crafting a new magical potion.

Mortimer was at the forbidden magical archives, researching ancient spells.

Quantum Mystics was In a hidden magical garden, tending to rare mystical herbs.

Who poisoned the Magical Elixir?

CLUE:

The poisoned magical elixir showed traces of a rare mystical toxin.

3. THE CRYPTO CONSPIRACY

Cryptocurrency mogul, Satoshi Cipher, was found dead in his high-security blockchain lab. The murder weapon is a tampered blockchain algorithm.

SUSPECTS

BILY

His aspirational blockchain programmer

VICTOR

His former business associate

CAPITAL

His Secretive enigmatic bitcoin investor

LOCATIONS

Bily was in the blockchain lab, working on a new cryptocurrency algorithm.

Victor was at his private vault, dealing with financial disputes.

Capital was in a secret cryptocurrency exchange office, monitoring investments.

Who tampered with blockchain algorithm used by Satoshi Cipher.

4. THE ARTISAN'S ANONYMITY

Master craftsman, Arturo Artisan, was found dead in his prestigious workshop. The murder weapon is a sabotaged sculpting tool.

SUSPECTS

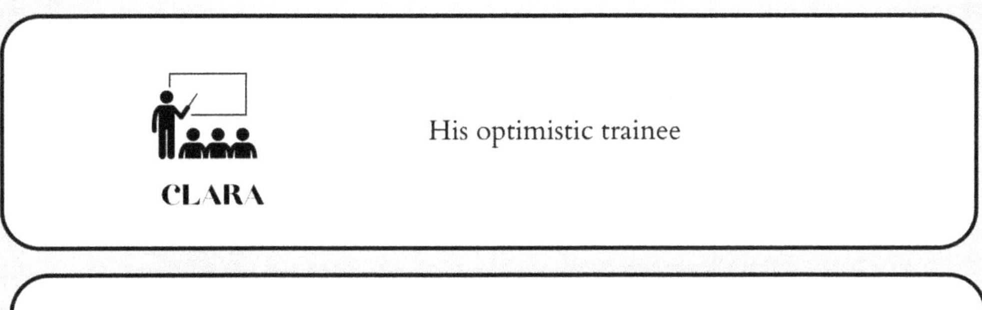

CLARA

His optimistic trainee

VINCENT VISIONARY

His estranged artistic rival

AESTHETICS

His enigmatic collector of fine arts

LOCATIONS

Clara was in the workshop, practicing sculpting techniques.

Vincent Visionary in his own art studio, preparing for a public art exhibition.

Aesthetics was in a hidden art gallery, evaluating potential acquisitions.

Who sabotaged sculpting tool?

CLUE:

Clara recently showcased a sculpture that outshone Arturo Artisan's masterpieces.

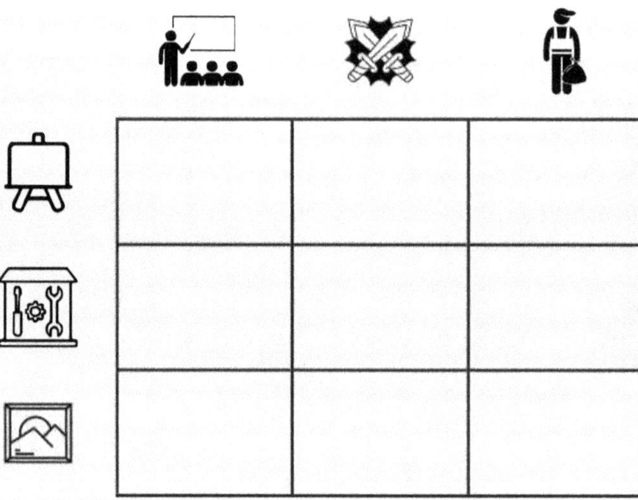

5. THE BOTANICAL BETRAYAL

Botanist extraordinaire, Dr. Flora Flair, was found dead in her lush botanical garden. The murder weapon is a poisoned rare orchid.

SUSPECTS

IVY

Her ambitious plant geneticist

REED

Her estranged botanical researcher

FLORA

Her mysterious plant supplier

LOCATIONS

Ivy was in the plant geneticist laboratory, experimenting with hybrid plant species.

Reed was in the private botanical library, researching ancient plant lore.

Flora was in a greenhouse facility, cultivating rare plants for supply.

Who poisoned the rare orchid used by Dr. Flora Flair?

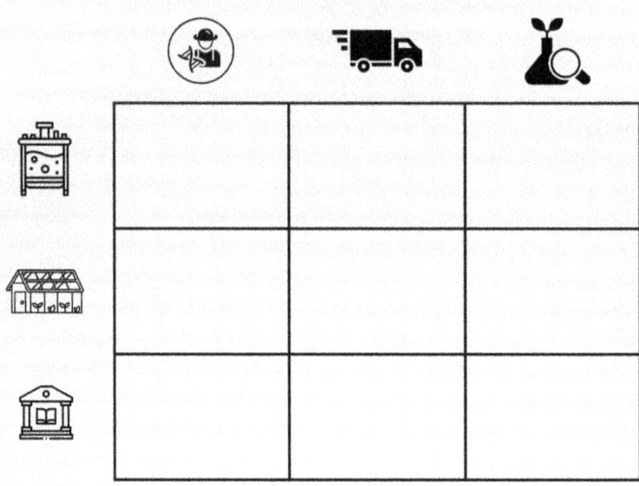

6. THE MUSICAL MISCHIEF

World-renowned composer, Maestro Melody, was found dead in his grand music hall. The murder weapon is a sabotaged conductor's baton.

SUSPECTS

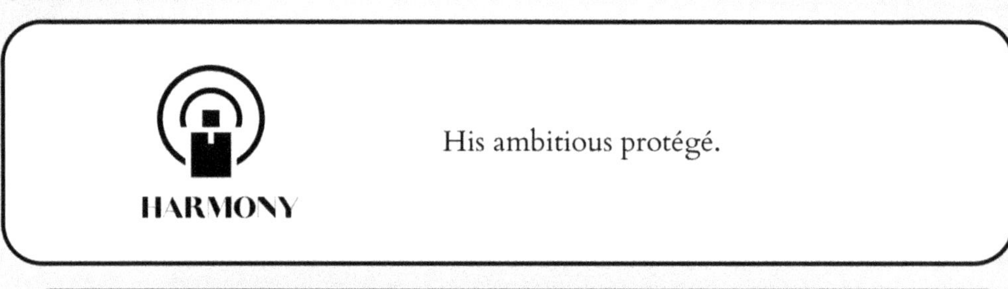

HARMONY

His ambitious protégé.

VIRTUOSO

His estranged musical collaborator

His mysterious music sponsor

LOCATIONS

Harmony was in the music studio, practicing a new composition.

Virtuoso was in a personal studio, working on a solo musical piece.

Crescendo was in a high-end music salon, evaluating potential investments.

Who sabotaged the conductor's baton used by Maestro Melody?

CLUE:

Harmony recently composed a musical piece that surpassed Maestro Melody's latest works.

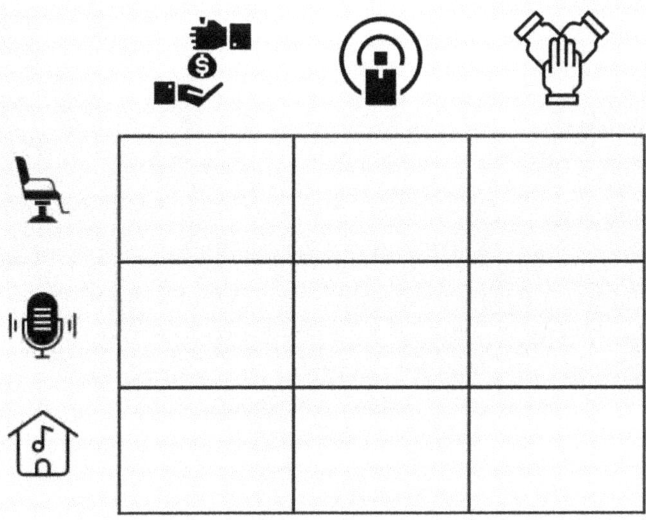

7. THE CULINARY CHEMYSTERY 

Celebrity chef, Gaston Gourmet, was found dead in his cutting-edge kitchen. The murder weapon is a poisoned molecular gastronomy dish.

SUSPECTS

SIMONE

His ambitious sous chef

MARCEL MORSEL

His estranged culinary rival

GASTRONOMY

his mysterious gourmet food supplier

LOCATIONS

Simone was in the experimental kitchen, creating a new molecular gastronomy dish.

Marcel Morsel was in a competing restaurant, preparing for a culinary competition.

Gastronomy In a gourmet food laboratory, developing exclusive culinary ingredients.

Who poisoned the molecular gastronomy dish?

The poisoned molecular gastronomy dish showed signs of intentional contamination.

8. THE TECH TITAN TAKEDOWN

Tech mogul, Dr. Axel Byte, was found dead in his state-of-the-art tech lab. The murder weapon is a sabotaged computer virus.

SUSPECTS

STELLA

His ambitious software engineer

VICTOR

His estranged tech competitor

His mysterious tech investment firm

LOCATIONS

Stella was in the software development lab, working on a revolutionary coding project.

Victor was in his tech company headquarters, strategizing ways to outshine Dr. Axel Byte.

Innovate was in a high-tech boardroom, discussing investments in cutting-edge tech projects.

Who sabotaged the computer virus used to infect Dr. Axel Byte's mainframe?

CLUE:

Quantum Innovate had financial interests in controlling the latest advancements in tech.

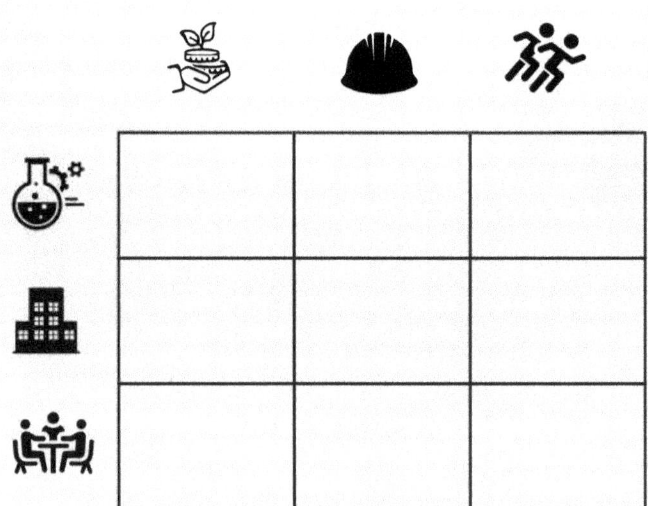

9. THE LITERARY LUNACY 

Bestselling author, Penelope Prose, was found dead in her private library. The murder weapon is a poisoned inkwell.

SUSPECTS

QUENTIN QUILL

Her ambitious literary agent

VICTOR VERB

Her estranged ex-husband

QUANTUM NOVELS

Her mysterious book publishing investor

LOCATIONS

Quentin Quill was in the literary agency office, negotiating book deals.

Victor Verb was in a rival publishing house, plotting to outshine Penelope Prose.

Quantum Novels was in a secret meeting room, discussing investments in the literary world.

Who poisoned the inkwell used by Penelope Prose?

10. THE ROBOTIC REBELLION

Inventor and robotics engineer, Dr. Amelia Automata, was found dead in her advanced robotics lab. The murder weapon is a reprogrammed robot.

SUSPECTS

MAX MECH

Her ambitious AI programmer

VICTOR VOLTAGE

Her estranged business partner

Her mysterious robotics investor

LOCATIONS

Max Mech In the AI programming room, developing advanced algorithms.

Victor Voltage in his own robotics workshop, working on a competing project.

Robotics Corp in a high-tech control center, overseeing investments in robotics

Who reprogrammed the robot used to attack Dr. Amelia Automata?

CLUE:

Robotics Corp had financial interests in controlling the latest advancements in robotics.

11. THE TIME-TRAVEL TURMOIL 

Renowned physicist, Dr. Tempus Temporal, was found dead in his time-travel research lab. The murder weapon is a tampered time-travel device.

SUSPECTS

CHRONOS CLOCKWORK

His ambitious assistant

PARADOX PRISM

His estranged time-travel collaborator

CHROMODYNAMICS

His mysterious time-travel investor

LOCATIONS

Chronos Clockwork in the time-travel lab, fine-tuning the temporal coordinates for an experiment.

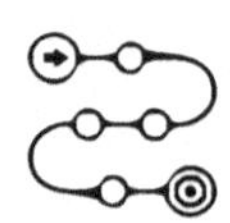

Paradox was in a parallel timeline, conducting unauthorized time-travel experiments.

Chromodynamics in a secure facility, monitoring investments in time-travel research.

Who tampered with the time-travel device used by Dr. Tempus Temporal?

12. THE HYPNOTIC HEIST

Renowned hypnotist, Dr. Maxwell Mesmer, was found dead after a high-profile stage performance. The murder weapon is a sabotaged hypnotic suggestion.

SUSPECTS

TRILBY — His ambitious apprentice

MYSTIQUE — His estranged former stage partner

His mysterious benefactor

LOCATIONS

Trilby was in the backstage area, practicing hypnotic techniques.

Mystole was in a competing entertainment venue, planning a comeback

Hypnosis Ltd was in a secretive office, discussing investments in hypnotic technologies.

Who sabotaged the hypnotic suggestion used by Dr. Maxwell Mesmer?

CLUE:

Hypnosis Ltd had a financial interest in controlling the intellectual property associated with hypnotic techniques.

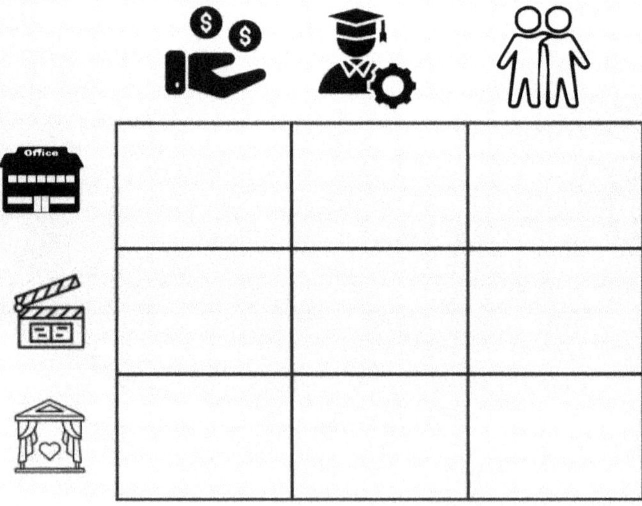

13. THE GALACTIC GAMBIT 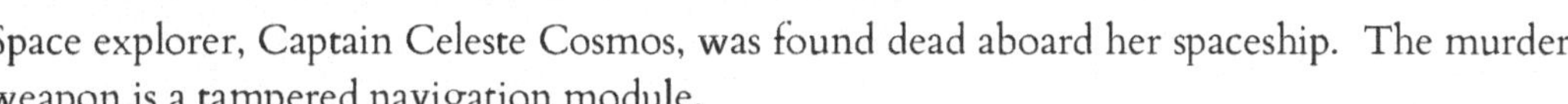

Space explorer, Captain Celeste Cosmos, was found dead aboard her spaceship. The murder weapon is a tampered navigation module.

SUSPECTS

NOVA

Her Ambitious Starship Navigator

ORION

Her Estranged Cosmic Entrepreneur

COSMIC VENTURES

Her Mysterious Space Exploration Sponsor

LOCATIONS

Nova was in the navigation control room, plotting a course through the cosmos.

Orion was in his private space station, strategizing ways to outshine Captain Cosmos.

Cosmic Ventures in a high-tech observatory, monitoring investments in space exploration.

Who tampered with the navigation module used by Captain Celeste Cosmos?

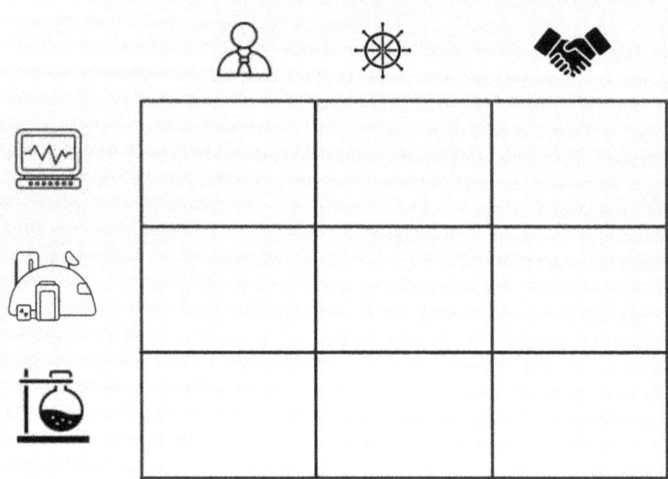

14. THE QUANTUM QUEST

Particle physicist, Dr. Quasar Quantum, was found dead in his cutting-edge quantum physics laboratory. The murder weapon is a manipulated quantum entanglement device.

SUSPECTS

QUARK

His Ambitious Quantum Physicist

FLUX

His Estranged Research Partner

His Mysterious Quantum Technology Investor

LOCATIONS

Quark was in the quantum physics lab, conducting experiments on particle entanglement.

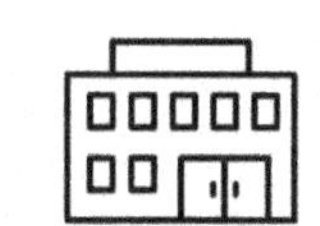

Flux was in a separate research facility, analyzing quantum phenomena.

Dynamics corp in a high-tech boardroom, discussing investments in quantum technology.

Who manipulated the quantum entanglement device used by Dr. Quasar Quantum.

CLUE:

Quantum Flux had a history of disagreements with Dr. Quantum over the interpretation of quantum data.

15. THE MUSICAL MYSTERIA 🔍

Famed composer, Maestro Crescendo, was found dead in his grand concert hall. The murder weapon is a poisoned baton.

SUSPECTS

ARIA ARPEGGIO

His Ambitious Musical Apprentice

VICTOR

His Estranged Symphony Conductor

SONORITY

His Mysterious Music Investment Company

LOCATIONS

Aria Arpeggio was in the music studio, composing a new symphony.

Victor was in a rival concert hall, preparing for a musical competition.

Sonority was in a high-tech music studio, discussing investments in classical music.

Who poisoned the conductor's baton used by Maestro Crescendo?

The poisoned conductor's baton showed signs of intentional tampering.

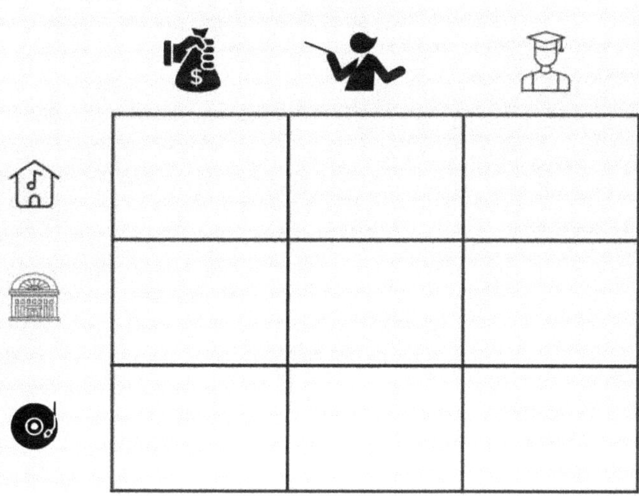

16. THE COSMIC CONUNDRUM 

Astrophysicist Dr. Stella Starlight was found dead in her observatory. The murder weapon is a manipulated telescope calibration system.

SUSPECTS

CELESTIAL

Her Ambitious Colleague

VORTEX

Her Estranged Rival Astrophysicist

Her Mysterious Cosmic Investor

LOCATIONS

Celestial was in the observatory control room, analyzing cosmic data.

Vortex was in his private observatory, studying celestial phenomena.

Quantum was in a futuristic office, discussing investments in cosmic research.

Who manipulated the telescope calibration system used by Dr. Stella Starlight?

CLUE:

Quantum Celestial Ventures had financial interests in controlling the latest advancements in cosmic research.

17. THE CYBERNETIC CONSPIRACY 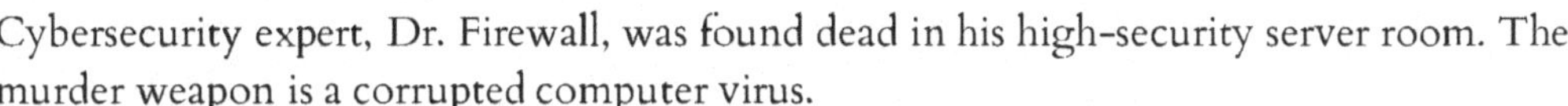

Cybersecurity expert, Dr. Firewall, was found dead in his high-security server room. The murder weapon is a corrupted computer virus.

SUSPECTS

CRYPTO SHIELD

His Ambitious Cybersecurity Analyst

VICTOR VIRAL

His Estranged Tech Entrepreneur Rival

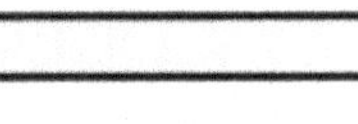

CYBERNETICS

His Mysterious Cyber-Investment Firm

LOCATIONS

Crypto shield was in the cybersecurity command center, monitoring network activity.

Victor Viral was in his tech innovation lab, developing new software applications.

Cybernetics was in a secure data facility, overseeing investments in cyber technology.

Who corrupted the computer virus injected into Dr. Firewall's main server?

18. THE GENETIC GAMBLE

Geneticist Dr. Helena Helix was found dead in her advanced genetics laboratory. The murder weapon is a sabotaged gene-editing tool.

SUSPECTS

Her Ambitious Genetic Researcher

Her Estranged Scientific Collaborator

Her Mysterious Genetic Investment Firm

LOCATIONS

Genome was in the genetics lab, experimenting with gene-editing techniques.

Victor Variant was in his own lab, working on a competing genetic research project.

Genomics in a futuristic boardroom, discussing investments in genetic research.

Who sabotaged the gene-editing tool used by Dr. Helena Helix?

CLUE:

Victor Variant had creative differences with Dr. Helix over the ethical use of gene-editing technologies.

19. THE CRYPTIC CIPHER

Renowned cryptographer, Dr. Enigma Encipher, was found dead in his encrypted message lab. The murder weapon is a tampered decryption algorithm.

SUSPECTS

CIPHER SLEUTH

His Ambitious Cryptography Analyst

VICTOR VAULT

His Estranged Encryption Rival

CRYPTICS

His Mysterious Cyber-Investment Firm

LOCATIONS

Cipher Sleuth was in the cryptography lab, decoding encrypted messages.

Victor Vault was in his private vault, working on a competing encryption algorithm.

Cryptics was in a high-security server room, overseeing investments in cryptography.

Who tampered with the decryption algorithm used by Dr. Enigma Encipher?

20. THE QUANTUM QUANDARY

Quantum physicist, Dr. Quantum Questor, was found dead in his advanced quantum research facility. The murder weapon is a manipulated quantum entanglement experiment.

SUSPECTS

THEORYMA

His Ambitious Quantum Theorist

VICTOR VORTEX

His Estranged Scientific Collaborator

DYNAMICS CORP

His Mysterious Quantum Investment Firm

LOCATIONS

Theoryma was in the quantum theory lab, exploring new theoretical concepts.

Victor Vortex was in his private quantum observatory conducting experiments on quantum phenomena

Dynamics corp was in a high-tech boardroom, discussing investments in quantum technology.

Who manipulated the quantum entanglement experiment used by Dr. Quantum Questor?

CLUE:

Quantum Dynamics Corp had financial interests in controlling the latest advancements in quantum technology.

21. THE ALIEN ANOMALY 🔍

Extraterrestrial researcher, Dr. Astro Alienor, was found dead in her research station on a distant planet. The murder weapon is a tampered alien artifact.

SUSPECTS

STELLA STARBEAM

Her Ambitious Astrobiologist

VICTOR VOYAGER

Her Estranged Intergalactic Explorer

GALACTIC VENTURES

Her Mysterious Alien Artifact Investor

LOCATIONS

Stella was in the astrobiology lab, studying extraterrestrial life forms.

Victor was in his own space exploration vessel, charting new courses in distant galaxies.

Galactic was in a cosmic artifact vault, discussing investments in alien discoveries.

Who tampered with the alien artifact discovered by Dr. Astro Alienor?

22. THE ROBOTIC REVOLUTION 

Robotics engineer, Dr. Metallica Machina, was found dead in her state-of-the-art robotics lab. The murder weapon is a sabotaged artificial intelligence (AI) chip.

SUSPECTS

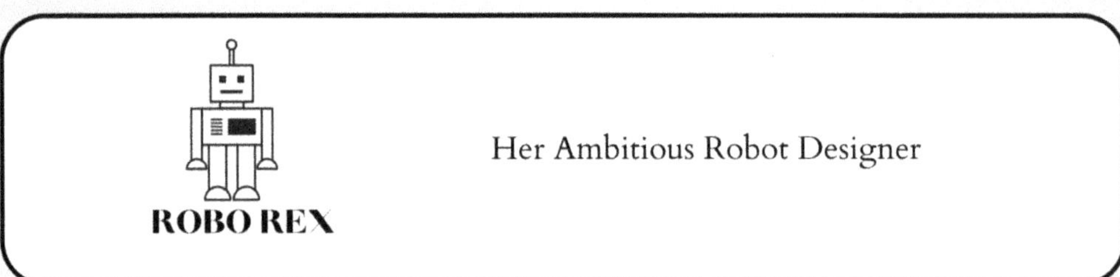

AUTOMATONS

Her Mysterious Robotics Investment Firm

LOCATIONS

Roborex was in the robotics lab, fine-tuning the programming for a new generation of robots.

Victor was in his private workshop, working on a competing AI chip.

Automatons was in a high-tech boardroom, discussing investments in advanced robotics.

Who sabotaged the AI chip used by Dr. Metallica Machina?

CLUE:

Robo Rex recently developed an AI chip that threatened to outperform Dr. Machina's robotics innovations.

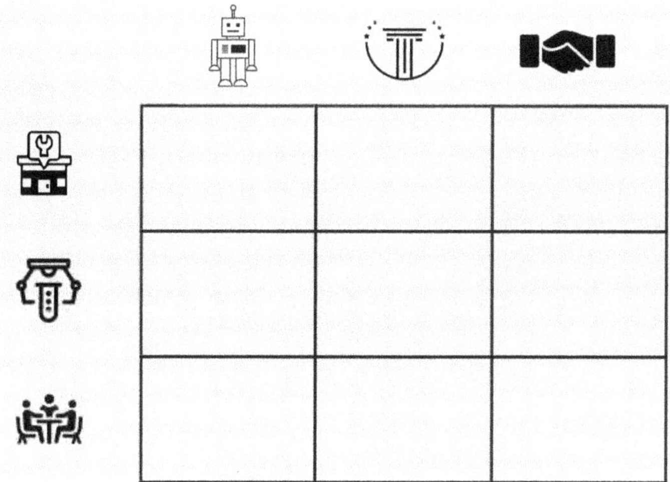

23. THE TIME-TWISTED TRAGEDY 

Temporal scientist, Dr. Tempus Temporalis, was found dead in his time-travel research lab. The murder weapon is a manipulated temporal displacement device.

SUSPECTS

TIMELOOP TURNER

His Ambitious Assistant

VICTOR VORTEX

His Estranged Temporal Researcher

TEMPORALITY VENTURES

His Mysterious Time-Tech Investor

LOCATIONS

Timeloop was in the temporal research lab, fine-tuning the temporal displacement calculations.

Victor was in his private time-travel observatory, conducting experiments on time anomalies.

Temporality was in a futuristic office, overseeing investments in temporal research.

Who manipulated the temporal displacement device used by Dr. Tempus Temporalis.

24. THE QUANTUM CONCLAVE 

Quantum physicist, Dr. Quasar Quandary, was found dead during a secret scientific conference. The murder weapon is a manipulated quantum experiment.

SUSPECTS

THEO THEOREM

His Ambitious Quantum Theorist

VICTOR VORTEX

His Estranged Research Partner

QUOTIENT SOLUTIONS

His Mysterious Quantum Investment Firm

LOCATIONS

Theo was in the secret quantum conference, presenting a groundbreaking theory.

Victor was in the quantum laboratory, conducting experiments on quantum phenomena.

Quotient was in a secure boardroom, discussing investments in quantum research.

Who manipulated the quantum experiment conducted by Dr. Quasar Quandary?

CLUE:

Theo Theorem recently proposed a quantum theory that threatened to overshadow Dr. Quandary's work.

25. THE HYPERSPACE HEIST

Renowned space explorer, Captain Celeste Celestial, was found dead on her spaceship during a hyperdrive test. The murder weapon is a manipulated hyperdrive system.

SUSPECTS

NOVA NAVIGANT

Her Ambitious Navigator

VICTOR VOYAGER

Her Estranged Cosmic Entrepreneur

CELESTIAL VENTURES

Her Mysterious Space Exploration Sponsor

LOCATIONS

Nova was in the navigation control room, calibrating the hyperdrive for the upcoming test.

Victor was in his private space station, developing a competing hyperdrive technology.

Celestial Venture was in a high-tech observatory, discussing investments in space exploration.

Who manipulated the hyperdrive system used by Captain Celeste Celestial?

26. THE MICROSCOPIC MYSTERY

Microbiologist Dr. Micro Molecule was found dead in his advanced microbiology lab. The murder weapon is a sabotaged bacterial culture.

SUSPECTS

MINI MICROBE

His Ambitious Lab Assistant

VICTOR VIRUS

His Estranged Research Collaborator

MICROCOSM SOLUTIONS

His Mysterious Microbiology Investment Firm

LOCATIONS

Mini was in the microbiology lab, conducting experiments on bacterial cultures.

Victor was in his own lab, working on a competing microbiological project.

Microcosmn a high-tech boardroom, discussing investments in microbiology.

Who sabotaged the bacterial culture used by Dr. Micro Molecule.

CLUE:

Mini Microbe recently developed a bacterial culture that threatened to outperform Dr. Micro Molecule's research.

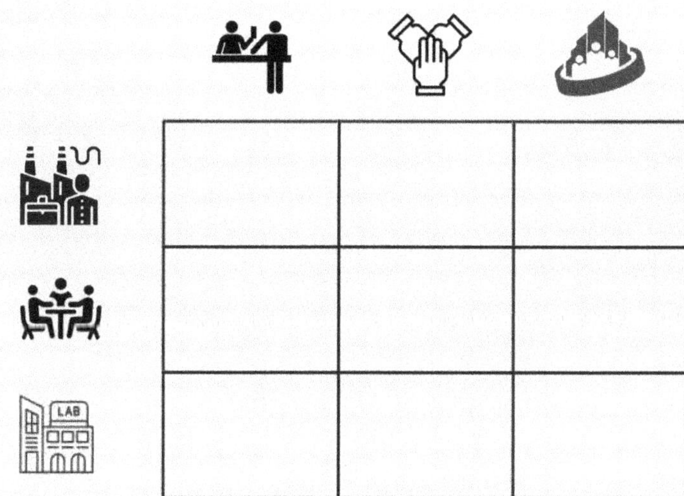

27. THE QUANTUM QUID PRO QUO 

Quantum physicist, Dr. Quasar Quotient, was found dead in his secret laboratory. The murder weapon is a tampered quantum experiment.

SUSPECTS

THEO THEOREM

His Ambitious Quantum Theorist

VORTEX

His Estranged Research Collaborator

QUANTA ENTERPRISES

His Mysterious Quantum Investment Firm

LOCATIONS

Theo was in the quantum theory lab, developing a revolutionary quantum theory.

Vortex was in the quantum laboratory, conducting experiments on quantum phenomena.

Quanta was in a secure boardroom, discussing investments in quantum research.

Who tampered with the quantum experiment conducted by Dr. Quasar Quotient?

28. THE COSMIC COLLUSION

Astrophysicist Dr. Celestia Cosmos was found dead in her observatory. The murder weapon
is a manipulated telescope calibration system.

SUSPECTS

STAR SEEKER

Her Ambitious Colleague

JAMES VORTEX

Her Estranged Rival Astrophysicist

CELESTIAL HOLDINGS

Her Mysterious Cosmic Investor

LOCATIONS

Star was in the observatory control room, analyzing cosmic data.

James was in his private observatory, studying celestial phenomena.

Celestial was in a futuristic office, discussing investments in cosmic research.

Who manipulated the telescope calibration system used by Dr. Celestia Cosmos?

CLUE:

Star Seeker recently made a groundbreaking cosmic discovery that surpassed Dr. Cosmos's work.

29. THE BIOCHEMICAL BETRAYAL 

Biochemist Dr. Bio Blazer was found dead in his advanced biochemical lab. The murder weapon is a sabotaged experimental enzyme.

SUSPECTS

GENE GENIUS

His Ambitious Lab Assistant

BRUCE VIRUS

His Estranged Research Collaborator

BIOSOLUTIONS

His mysterious biochemical investment firm

LOCATIONS

Gene was in the biochemical lab, conducting experiments on enzyme development.

Bruce was in his own lab, working on a competing biochemical project.

Biosolutions was in a high-tech boardroom, discussing investments in biochemical research.

Who sabotaged the experimental enzyme used by Dr. Bio Blazer?

Gene Genius recently developed an experimental enzyme that threatened to outperform Dr. Blazer's research.

30. THE QUANTUM QUAGMIRE

Quantum physicist, Dr. Quark Quantum, was found dead in his secret laboratory. The murder weapon is a tampered quantum experiment.

SUSPECTS

THEO THEOREM

His Ambitious Quantum Theorist

DAVE VORTEX

His Estranged Research Collaborator

His Mysterious Quantum Investment Firm

LOCATIONS

Theo was in the quantum theory lab, developing a revolutionary quantum theory.

Dave was in the quantum laboratory, conducting experiments on quantum phenomena.

Quotient was in a secure boardroom, discussing investments in quantum research.

Who tampered with the quantum experiment conducted by Dr. Quark Quantum?

CLUE:

Dave Vortex had a history of fierce competition and academic disputes with Dr. Quantum.

31. THE CYBERNETIC CONSPIRACY II

Cybersecurity expert, Dr. Firewalla, was found dead in her high-security server room. The murder weapon is a corrupted firewall system.

SUSPECTS

CRYPTO CIPHER

Her Ambitious Cybersecurity Analyst

DAVID VIRUS

Her Estranged Tech Entrepreneur Rival

CYBERNETICS CORP

Her mysterious cyber-investment firm

LOCATIONS

Crypto was in the cybersecurity command center, monitoring network activity.

David was in his tech innovation lab, developing new software applications.

Cybernetics was in a secure data facility, overseeing investments in cyber technology.

Who corrupted the firewall system used by Dr. Firewalla?

32. THE GENETIC GAMBIT II

Geneticist Dr. Helixa was found dead in her advanced genetics laboratory. The murder
weapon is a sabotaged gene-editing tool.

SUSPECTS

GENE GENOME

Her ambitious genetic researcher

VICTOR VARIANT

Her Estranged Scientific Collaborator

Her Mysterious Genetic Investment Firm

LOCATIONS

Gene was in the genetics lab, experimenting with gene-editing techniques.

Victor was in his own lab, working on a competing genetic research project.

Genomics was in a futuristic boardroom, discussing investments in genetic research

Who sabotaged the gene-editing tool used by Dr. Helixa?

CLUE:

Gene Genome recently developed a revolutionary gene-editing technique that threatened Dr. Helixa's genetic innovations.

33. THE CRYPTIC CIPHER II

Renowned cryptographer, Dr. Enigma Encipher, was found dead in his encrypted message lab. The murder weapon is a tampered encryption algorithm.

SUSPECTS

CRYPTO DECIPHER

His Ambitious Cryptography Analyst

JANE VAULT

His estranged encryption rival

CRYPTICS CORP

His Mysterious Cryptography Investment Firm

LOCATIONS

Crypto was in the cryptography lab, decoding encrypted messages.

Jane was in his private vault, working on a competing encryption algorithm.

Cryptics was in a high-security server room, overseeing investments in cryptography.

Who tampered with encryption algorithm used by Dr. Enigma Encipher?

34. THE TECHNOLOGICAL TREACHERY 

Technology innovator, Dr. Techno Titan, was found dead in his cutting-edge tech lab. The murder weapon is a sabotaged prototype drone.

SUSPECTS

VICTOR VOLTAGE

His Ambitious Tech Developer

CYBER CIPHER

His Estranged Business Partner

His Mysterious Tech Investment Firm

LOCATIONS

Victor was in the tech lab, working on a prototype drone for a new project.

Cyber was in the tech development center, exploring new applications for drone technology.

Quantum was in a high-tech boardroom, discussing investments in technological research.

Who sabotaged the prototype drone used by Dr. Techno Titan?

CLUE:

Victor Voltage recently developed a drone prototype that threatened to outperform Dr. Techno Titan's innovations.

35. THE QUANTUM QUANDARY II

Quantum physicist, Dr. Quasar Quandary, was found dead in his secret laboratory. The murder weapon is a tampered quantum experiment.

SUSPECTS

THEO THEOREM

His Ambitious Quantum Theorist

VICTOR VORTEX

His Estranged Research Partner

QUOTIENT HOLDINGS

His Mysterious Quantum Investment Firm

LOCATIONS

Theo was in the quantum theory lab, developing a revolutionary quantum theory.

Victor was in the quantum laboratory, conducting experiments on quantum phenomena.

Quotient was in a secure boardroom, discussing investments in quantum research.

Who tampered with the quantum experiment conducted by Dr. Quasar Quandary?

CLUE:

Quotient Holdings had financial interests in controlling the latest advancements in quantum research.

36. THE ENIGMATIC ESCAPE 

Renowned escapologist, Illusionist Ingrid, was found dead in her locked escape room. The murder weapon is a rigged escape contraption.

SUSPECTS

MYSTIC MIRAGE

Her Ambitious Apprentice

VICTOR VANISH

Her Estranged Rival Magician

Her Mysterious Magic Investment Firm

LOCATIONS

Mystic was in the magic workshop, practicing new escape techniques.

Victor was in his private magic theater, preparing for a grand illusion show.

Illusions was in a high-tech boardroom, discussing investments in magical performances.

Who rigged the escape contraption used by Illusionist Ingrid?

CLUE:

Mystic Mirage recently developed an escape contraption that threatened to outshine Illusionist Ingrid's tricks.

37. THE QUANTUM QUEST II: THE LOST EQUATION 

Mathematician Dr. Matrix Maven was found dead in his secluded mathematics research center. The murder weapon is a tampered mathematical proof.

SUSPECTS

LAX THEOREM

His Ambitious Protégé

VICTOR VARIABLES

His Estranged Mathematical Collaborator

EQUATIONS VENTURES

His Mysterious Math Investment Firm

LOCATIONS

Lax was in the math research center, exploring new mathematical concepts

Victor was in his own secluded math study, working on a competing mathematical proof.

Equations was in a high-tech boardroom, discussing investments in mathematical research.

Who tampered with the mathematical proof used by Dr. Matrix Maven?

Lax Theorem recently proposed a mathematical proof that threatened to overshadow Dr. Maven's work.

38. THE LITERARY LABYRINTH

Best-selling author, Penelope Puzzler, was found dead in her private library. . The murder weapon is a poisoned quill.

SUSPECTS

VICTOR VERSIFIER

Her Ambitious Literary Protégé

MYSTERY MAVEN

Her Estranged Author Competitor

QUILLS CONSORTIUM

Her Mysterious Publishing Investment Firm

LOCATIONS

Victor was in the writing studio, working on a new literary masterpiece.

Mystery was in her own literary haven, crafting a riveting mystery novel.

Quills was in a high-tech literary agency, discussing investments in publishing.

Who poisoned the quill used by Penelope Puzzler?

CLUE:

Mystery Maven had creative differences with Puzzler over the direction of their writing styles.

39. THE ASTRAL ANOMALY

Astrologer extraordinaire, Celestia Starlight, was found dead in her celestial observatory. The murder weapon is a manipulated celestial chart.

SUSPECTS

NOVA NEBULA

Her Ambitious Apprentice

DANIEL VORTEX

Her Estranged Cosmic Mystic Rival

HOROSCOPES INC

Her Mysterious Astrological Investment Firm

LOCATIONS

Nova was in the astrological observatory, studying celestial patterns.

Daniel was in his private cosmic sanctuary, interpreting cosmic signs.

Horoscopes was in a futuristic office, discussing investments in astrological research.

Who manipulated the celestial chart used by Celestia Starlight?

40. THE QUANTUM QUANTUM LEAP

Quantum physicist, Dr. Quark Quantumleap, was found dead in his secret laboratory. The murder weapon is a tampered quantum experiment.

SUSPECTS

THEOREMLEAP

His Ambitious Quantum Theorist

VICTOR VORTEXLEAP

His estranged research partner

His Mysterious Quantum Investment Firm

LOCATIONS

Theoremileap was in the quantum theory lab, developing a revolutionary quantum theory.

Victor was in the quantum laboratory, conducting experiments on quantum phenomena.

Quotient was in a secure boardroom, discussing investments in quantum research.

Who tampered with the quantum experiment conducted by Dr. Quark Quantumleap?

CLUE:

Victor Vortexleap had a history of fierce competition and academic disputes with Dr. Quantumleap.

41. THE VANISHING ACT

Illusionist extraordinaire, Enchanting Elara, was found dead in her grand theater. The murder weapon is a sabotaged disappearing act.

SUSPECTS

VICTOR VANISH

Her Ambitious Understudy

MYSTICAL MIRAGE

Her Estranged Rival Illusionist

ILLUSIONS UNLIMITED

Her Mysterious Magic Investment Firm

LOCATIONS

Victor was in the backstage illusion room, practicing a disappearing act.

Mystical was in his own mystical realm, crafting illusions for his upcoming show.

Illusion was in a high-tech theater control room, discussing investments in magical performances.

Who sabotaged the disappearing act used by Enchanting Elara?

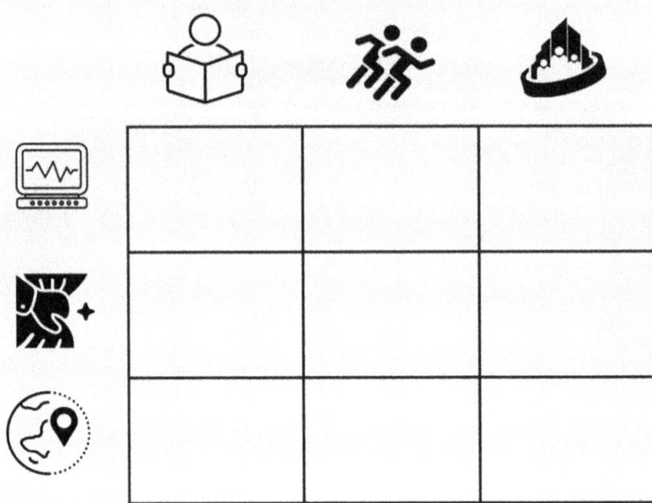

42. THE TECHNO-TREACHERY II

Tech mogul, Dr. Byte Bender, was found dead in his state-of-the-art tech lab. The murder weapon is a manipulated AI algorithm.

SUSPECTS

His Ambitious Tech Prodigy

KELLY VOLTAGE

His Estranged Business Partner

CYBER CIPHER

His Mysterious Tech Investment Firm

LOCATIONS

Kelly was in the tech lab, fine-tuning an advanced AI algorithm.

Cyber was in the cybernetic research center, working on a competing AI project.

Innovations was in a futuristic office, discussing investments in technological research.

Who manipulated the AI algorithm used by Dr. Byte Bender?

CLUE:

Kelly Voltage recently developed an AI algorithm that threatened to outperform Dr. Byte Bender's innovations.

43. THE CLONE CONSPIRACY 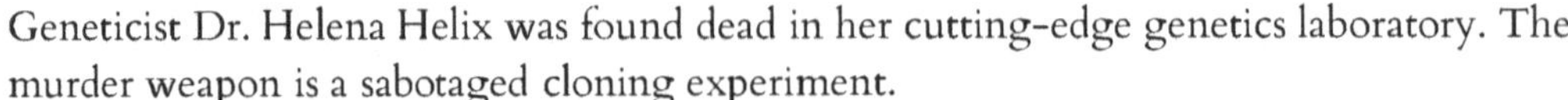

Geneticist Dr. Helena Helix was found dead in her cutting-edge genetics laboratory. The murder weapon is a sabotaged cloning experiment.

SUSPECTS

GENE GENIE

Her Ambitious Genetic Researcher

VICTOR VARIANT

Her Estranged Scientific Collaborator

GENOMICS HOLDINGS

Her Mysterious Genetic Investment Firm

LOCATIONS

Gene was in the genetics lab, experimenting with cloning techniques.

Victor was in his own lab, working on a competing cloning research project.

Genomics was in a futuristic boardroom, discussing investments in genetic research.

Who sabotaged the cloning experiment used by Dr. Helena Helix?

CLUE:

Lax Theorem recently proposed a mathematical proof that threatened to overshadow Dr. Maven's work.

44. TIME LOOP PARADOX 

Quantum physicist, Dr. Quasar Quirk, was found dead in his time-bending research lab. The murder weapon is a manipulated time loop device.

SUSPECTS

TEMPORAL TINKERER

His Ambitious Assistant

VICTOR VORTEX

His Estranged Temporal Researcher

LOCATIONS

Tinkerer was in the temporal research lab, fine-tuning the time loop device.

Victor was in his private time-travel observatory, conducting experiments on time anomalies.

Temporal was in a futuristic office, overseeing investments in temporal research.

Who manipulated the time loop device used by Dr. Quasar Quirk?

CLUE:

Temporal Tinkerer recently developed a time loop device that threatened Dr. Quirk's work.

45. COSMIC CODES

Astrophysicist Dr. Celestia Cipher was found dead in her celestial observatory. The murder weapon is a manipulated set of encrypted cosmic codes.

SUSPECTS

VICTOR VECTOR

Her Ambitious Data Analyst

STELLAR SCHOLAR

Her Estranged Rival Astrophysicist

CELESTIAL HOLDINGS

Her Mysterious Cosmic Investor

LOCATIONS

Victor was in the data analysis room, decoding cosmic signals.

Stellar was in his private observatory, analyzing celestial phenomena.

Celestial was in a futuristic office, discussing investments in cosmic research.

Who manipulated the set of encrypted cosmic codes used by Dr. Celestia Cipher?

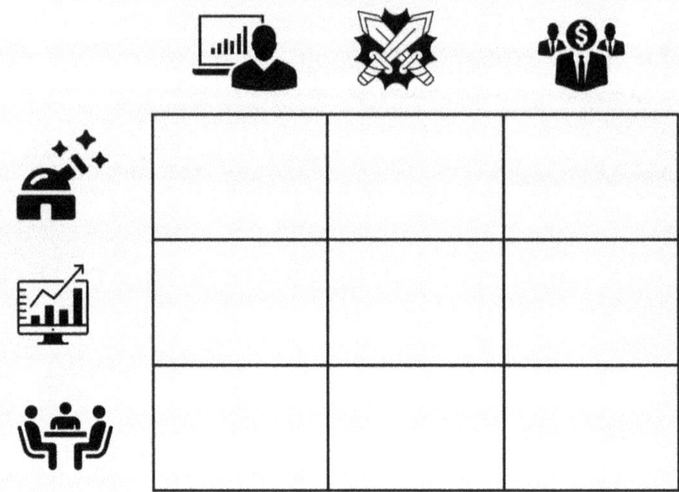

46. THE PARADOX PROPHECY

Quantum physicist, Dr. Quark Quantumquest, was found dead in his secret laboratory. The murder weapon is a tampered quantum experiment with a paradoxical twist.

SUSPECTS

THEOREMQUEST

His Ambitious Quantum Theorist

VORTEXQUEST

His Estranged Research Partner

His Mysterious Quantum Investment Firm

LOCATIONS

Theorem was in the quantum theory lab, developing a revolutionary quantum theory.

Vortex was in the quantum laboratory, conducting experiments on quantum phenomena.

Quotient was in a secure boardroom, discussing investments in quantum research.

Who tampered with the quantum experiment with a paradoxical twist conducted by Dr. Quark Quantumquest?

CLUE:

Vortexquest had a history of fierce competition and academic disputes with Dr. Quantumquest.

47. DIGITAL DISRUPTION

Tech innovator, Dr. Techno Tinkerer, was found dead in his cutting-edge tech lab. The murder weapon is a manipulated digital code disrupting key systems.

SUSPECTS

BEN VOLTAGE

His Ambitious Tech Developer

CYBER CIPHER

His Estranged Tech Entrepreneur Rival

TECH NEXUS

His Mysterious Tech Investment Firm

LOCATIONS

Ben was in the tech lab, coding a new software application.

In the tech development center, working on a competing tech project.

Tech Nexus was in a futuristic office, discussing investments in technological research.

Who manipulated the digital code disrupting key systems used by Dr. Techno Tinkerer?

CLUE:
Ben Voltage recently developed a digital code disrupting key systems that threatened to outperform Dr. Techno Tinkerer's innovations.

48. DNA DECEPTION

Bioengineer Dr. Gene Genesis was found dead in his advanced biotech lab. The murder weapon is a manipulated gene-editing tool with altered DNA sequences.

SUSPECTS

VICTOR VARIANT

His Ambitious Lab Assistant

GENOME GURU

His Estranged Genetic Collaborator

BIOGENESIS CORP

His Mysterious Biotech Investment Firm

LOCATIONS

Victor was in the biotech lab, experimenting with gene-editing techniques.

Genome was in his own lab, working on a competing genetic research project.

Biogenesis was in a futuristic boardroom, discussing investments in biotech research.

Who manipulated the gene-editing tool with altered DNA sequences used by Dr. Gene Genesis?

CLUE:

Victor Variant recently developed a gene-editing tool with altered DNA sequences that threatened Dr. Gene Genesis's genetic breakthroughs.

49. DIMENSIONAL DISARRAY 

Quantum physicist, Dr. Quasar Quandary, was found dead in his secret laboratory. The murder weapon is a tampered quantum experiment causing dimensional disarray.

SUSPECTS

THEO THEOREM

His Ambitious Quantum Theorist

VICTOR VORTEX

His Estranged Research Partner

QUOTIENT NEXUS

His Mysterious Quantum Investment Firm

LOCATIONS

Theo was in the quantum theory lab, developing a revolutionary quantum theory.

Victor was in the quantum laboratory, conducting experiments on quantum phenomena.

Quotient was in a secure boardroom, discussing investments in quantum research.

Who tampered with the quantum experiment causing dimensional disarray conducted by Dr. Quasar Quandary?

Victor Vortex had a history of fierce competition and academic disputes with Dr. Quandary.

50. QUANTUM HACKING HEIST

Cybersecurity expert, Dr. Firewalla, was found dead in her high-security server room. The murder weapon is a manipulated quantum hacking tool.

SUSPECTS

CRYPTO CIPHER

Her Ambitious Cybersecurity Analyst

VICTOR VIRUS

Her Estranged Tech Entrepreneur Rival

Her Mysterious Cyber-Investment Firm

LOCATIONS

Crypto was in the cybersecurity command center, monitoring network activity.

Victor was in his tech innovation lab, developing new quantum hacking tools.

Cybersec was in a secure data facility, overseeing investments in cyber technology.

Who manipulated the quantum hacking tool used by Dr. Firewalla?

CLUE:

Victor Virus had creative differences with Dr. Firewalla over the direction of their cybersecurity projects.

THE

END

SOLUTIONS

1.

The murderer is Lily. The argument with Evelyn gave her the motive, and her proximity to the victim made it possible for her to poison the cocktail.

2.

The murderer is Mortimer. His motive was linked to his desire for forbidden magical knowledge, and poisoning the elixir was a way to eliminate Professor Alchemy, who stood in the way of Mortimer's ambitions.

3.

The murderer is Bily. Her motive was linked to professional rivalry, and tampering with the block chain algorithm was a way to eliminate Satoshi Cipher and take control of the cryptocurrency market.

4.

The murderer is Mortimer. His motive was linked to his desire for forbidden magical knowledge, and poisoning the elixir was a way to eliminate Professor Alchemy, who stood in the way of Mortimer's ambitions.

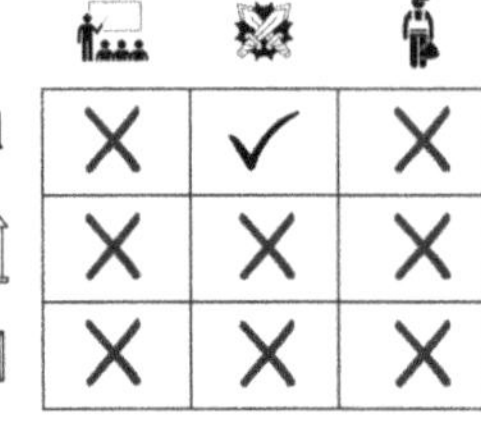

5.

The murderer is Ivy. Her motive was linked to professional rivalry, and poisoning the rare orchid was a way to eliminate Dr. Flora Flair, ensuring Ivy's dominance in the field of plant genetics.

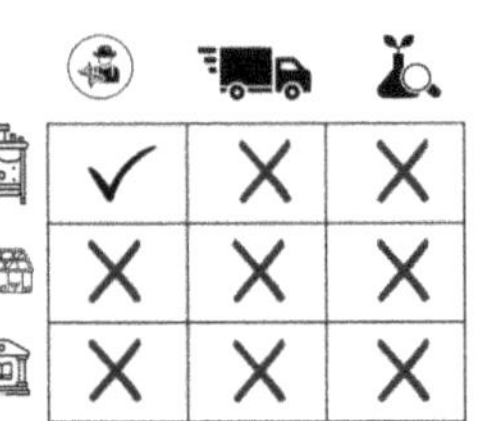

6.

The murderer is Virtuoso. His motive was linked to artistic rivalry, and sabotaging the conductor's baton was a way to eliminate Maestro Melody, allowing Victor to take center stage in the world of classical music.

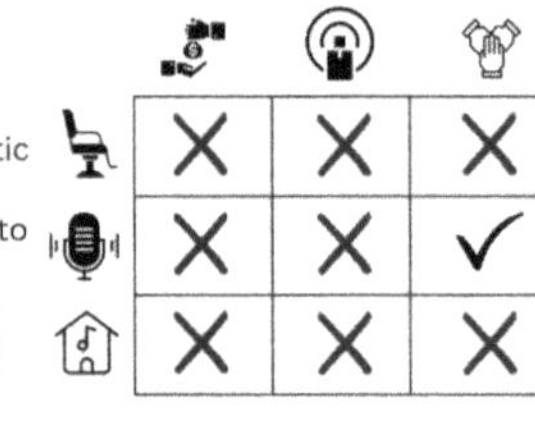

7.

The murderer is Simone. Her motive was linked to culinary rivalry, and poisoning the molecular gastronomy dish was a way to eliminate Gaston Gourmet, securing Simone's place as the leading figure in the world of molecular gastronomy.

8.

The murderer is Mortimer. His motive was linked to his desire for forbidden magical knowledge, and poisoning the elixir was a way to eliminate Professor Alchemy, who stood in the way of Mortimer's ambitions.

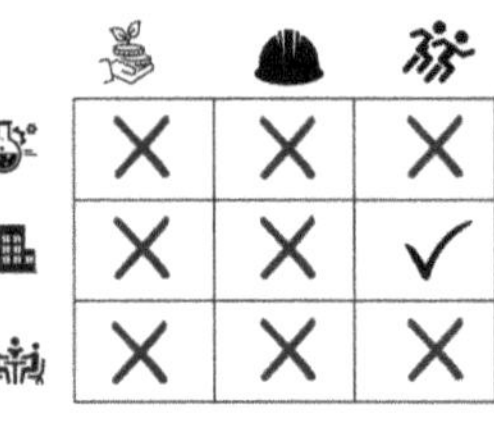

9.

The murderer is Quentin Quill. His motive was linked to financial gain and the desire to represent a more profitable author. Poisoning the inkwell was a clever way to eliminate Penelope Prose and secure a lucrative deal with the new author.

10.

The murderer is Victor Voltage. His motive was linked to professional rivalry, and reprogramming the robot was a way to eliminate Dr. Amelia Automata and take control of the groundbreaking robotics project.

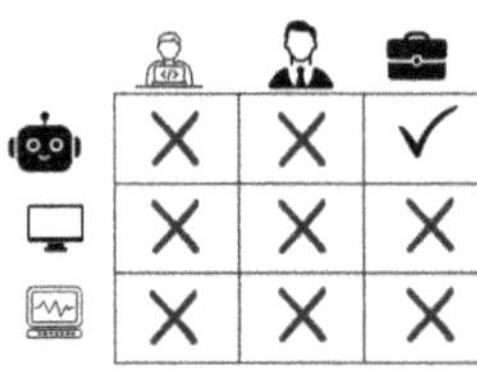

11.

The murderer is Paradox Prism. The motive was linked to disagreements over the ethical use of time travel, and tampering with the device was a way to prevent the success of Dr. Temporal's groundbreaking research.

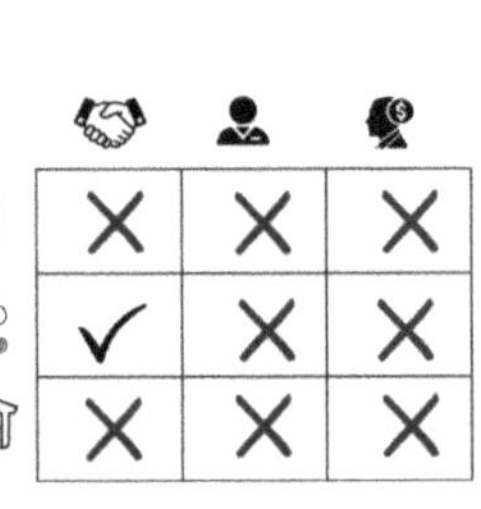

12.

The murderer is Mirage Mystique. The motive was linked to a desire for a successful comeback, and sabotaging the hypnotic suggestion was a way to eliminate Dr. Maxwell Mesmer and regain the spotlight.

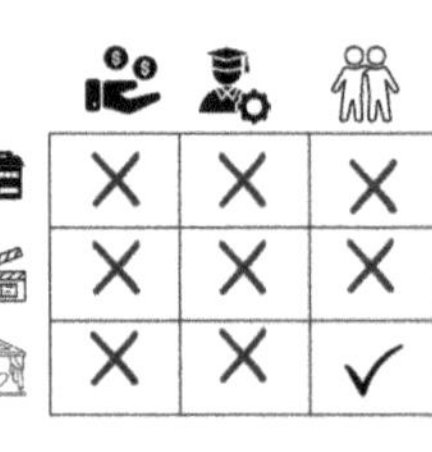

13.

The murderer is Nova . The motive was linked to professional rivalry, and tampering with the navigation module was a way to eliminate Captain Celeste Cosmos and establish Nova as the lead navigator in space exploration.

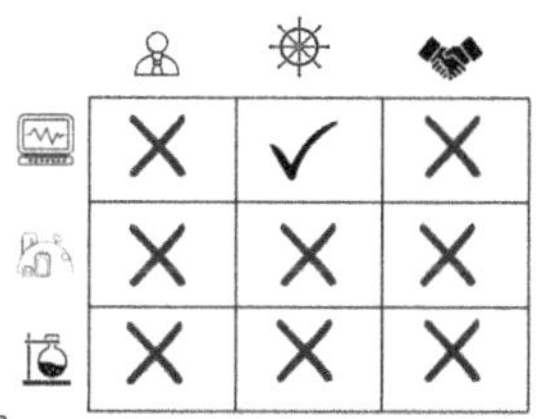

14.

The murderer is Flux. The motive was linked to unresolved scientific disputes, and manipulating the quantum entanglement device was a way to eliminate Dr. Quasar Quantum and ensure Quantum Flux's dominance in quantum physics.

15.

The murderer is Aria Arpeggio. The motive was linked to a desire for musical recognition, and poisoning the conductor's baton was a way to eliminate Maestro Crescendo and establish Aria as the preeminent composer.

16.

The murderer is Celestial Explorer. The motive was linked to professional rivalry, and manipulating the telescope calibration system was a way to eliminate Dr. Stella Starlight and ensure Celestial Explorer's dominance in the field of astrophysics.

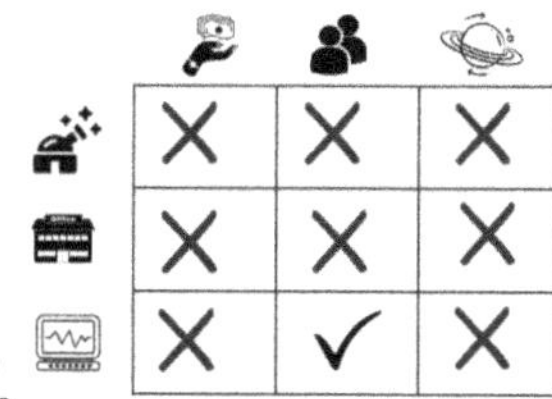

17.

The murderer is Crypto Shield. The motive was linked to professional rivalry, and injecting the corrupted computer virus was a way to eliminate Dr. Firewall and establish Crypto Shield's dominance in the field of cybersecurity.

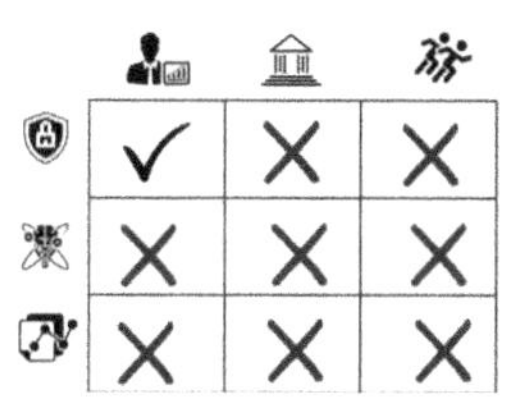

18.

The murderer is Victor Variant. The motive was linked to ethical disagreements, and sabotaging the gene-editing tool was a way to eliminate Dr. Helena Helix and assert control over the direction of genetic research.

19.

The murderer is Cipher Sleuth. The motive was linked to professional rivalry, and tampering with the decryption algorithm was a way to eliminate Dr. Enigma Encipher and establish Cipher Sleuth as the leading cryptographer.

20.

The murderer is Victor Vortex. The motive was linked to unresolved scientific disputes, and manipulating the quantum entanglement experiment was a way to eliminate Dr. Quantum Questor and ensure Victor Vortex's dominance in the field of quantum physics.

21.

The murderer is Galactic Ventures. The motive was linked to financial interests, and tampering with the alien artifact was a way to eliminate Dr. Astro Alienor and gain control over valuable extraterrestrial discoveries.

22.

The murderer is Victor Voltage. The motive was linked to professional rivalry, and sabotaging the AI chip was a way to eliminate Dr. Metallica Machina and assert control over the future of robotics technology.

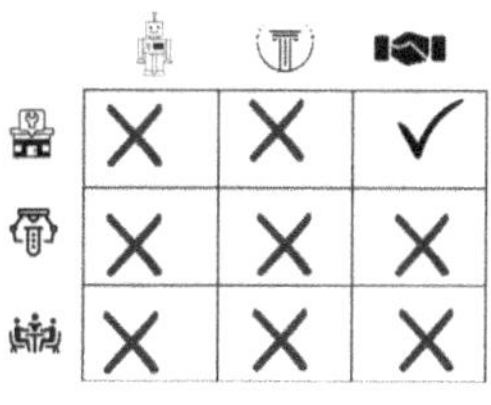

23.

The murderer is Timeloop Turner. The motive was linked to professional rivalry, and manipulating the temporal displacement device was a way to eliminate Dr. Tempus Temporalis and secure Timeloop Turner's position as the leading temporal scientist.

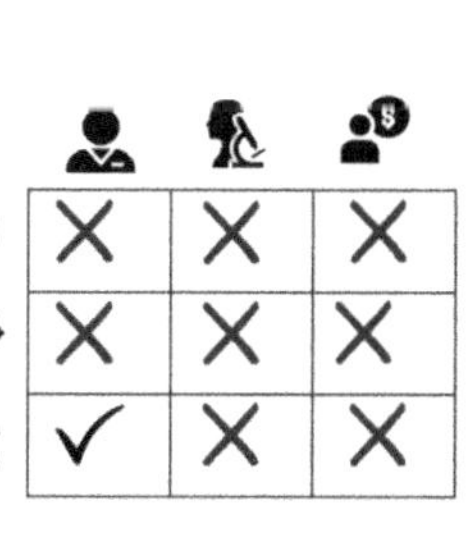

24.

The murderer is Victor Vortex. The motive was linked to unresolved scientific disputes, and manipulating the quantum experiment was a way to eliminate Dr. Quasar Quandary and ensure Victor Vortex's dominance in the field of quantum physics.

25.

The murderer is Nova Navigant. The motive was linked to professional rivalry, and manipulating the hyperdrive system was a way to eliminate Captain Celeste Celestial and regain a leading position in space exploration.

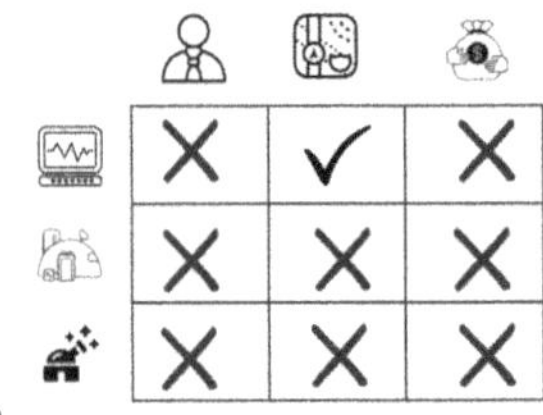

26.

The murderer is Victor Virus. The motive was linked to professional rivalry, and sabotaging the bacterial culture was a way to eliminate Dr. Micro Molecule and assert control over the field of microbiology.

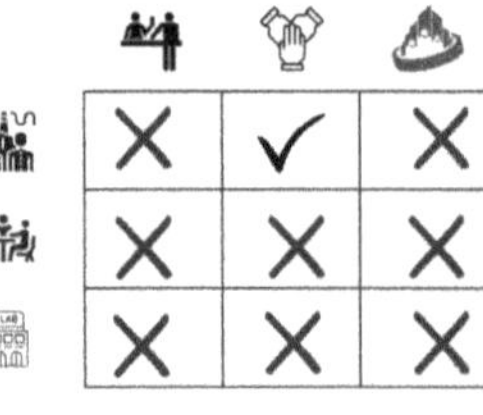

27.

The murderer is Theo Theorem. The motive was linked to professional rivalry, and tampering with the quantum experiment was a way to eliminate Dr. Quasar Quotient and establish Theo Theorem as the leading quantum theorist.

28.

The murderer is Star Seeker. The motive was linked to professional rivalry, and manipulating the telescope calibration system was a way to eliminate Dr. Celestia Cosmos and ensure Star Seeker's dominance in the field of astrophysics.

29.

The murderer is Bruce Virus. The motive was linked to professional rivalry, and sabotaging the experimental enzyme was a way to eliminate Dr. Bio Blazer and assert control over the field of biochemistry.

30.

The murderer is Dave Vortex. The motive was linked to unresolved scientific disputes, and tampering with the quantum experiment was a way to eliminate Dr. Quark Quantum and ensure Victor Vortex's dominance in the field of quantum physics.

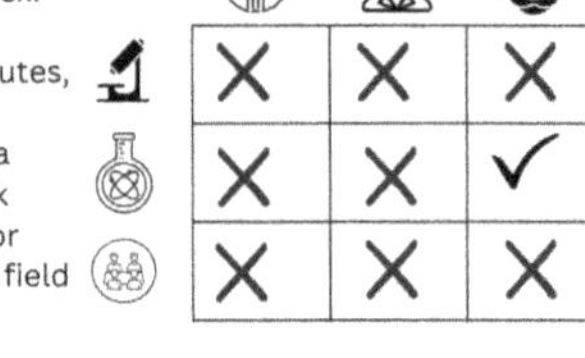

31.

The murderer is Crypto Cipher. The motive was linked to professional rivalry, and corrupting the firewall system was a way to eliminate Dr. Firewalla and assert control over the field of cybersecurity.

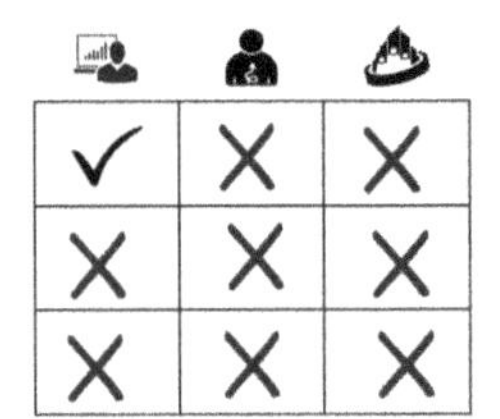

32.

The murderer is Victor Variant. The motive was linked to ethical disagreements, and sabotaging the gene-editing tool was a way to eliminate Dr. Helixa and assert control over the direction of genetic research.

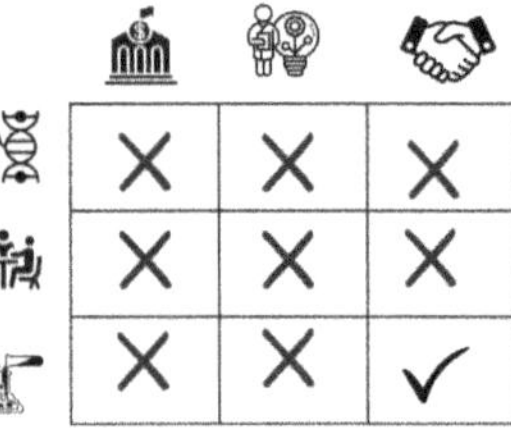

33.

The murderer is Jane Vault. The motive was linked to professional rivalry, and tampering with the encryption algorithm was a way to eliminate Dr. Enigma Encipher and establish Victor Vault as the leading cryptographer.

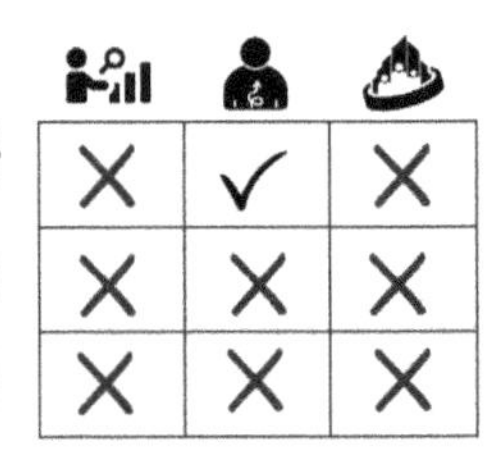

34.

The murderer is Cyber Cipher. The motive was linked to professional rivalry, and sabotaging the prototype drone was a way to eliminate Dr. Techno Titan and assert control over the future of technology.

35.

The murderer is Theo Theorem. The motive was linked to professional rivalry, and tampering with the quantum experiment was a way to eliminate Dr. Quasar Quandary and establish Theo Theorem as the leading quantum theorist.

36.

The murderer is Mystic Mirage. The motive was linked to professional rivalry, and rigging the escape contraption was a way to eliminate Illusionist Ingrid and establish Mystic Mirage as the leading escapologist.

37.

The murderer is Victor Variables. The motive was linked to unresolved mathematical disputes, and tampering with the mathematical proof was a way to eliminate Dr. Matrix Maven and ensure Victor Variables' dominance in the field of mathematics.

38.

The murderer is Mystery Maven. The motive was linked to professional rivalry, and poisoning the quill was a way to eliminate Penelope Puzzler and establish Mystery Maven as the leading author in the literary world.

39.

The murderer is Nova Nebula. The motive was linked to professional rivalry, and manipulating the celestial chart was a way to eliminate Celestia Starlight and establish Nova Nebula as the leading astrologer.

40.

The murderer is Theo Theoremleap. The motive was linked to professional rivalry, and tampering with the quantum experiment was a way to eliminate Dr. Quark Quantumleap and establish Theo Theoremleap as the leading quantum theorist.

41.

The murderer is Mystical Mirage. The motive was linked to professional rivalry, and sabotaging the disappearing act was a way to eliminate Enchanting Elara and establish Mystical Mirage as the leading illusionist.

42.

The murderer is Cyber Cipher. The motive was linked to professional rivalry, and manipulating the AI algorithm was a way to eliminate Dr. Byte Bender and assert control over the future of AI technology.

43.

The murderer is Victor Variant. The motive was linked to ethical disagreements, and sabotaging the cloning experiment was a way to eliminate Dr. Helena Helix and assert control over the field of genetic cloning.

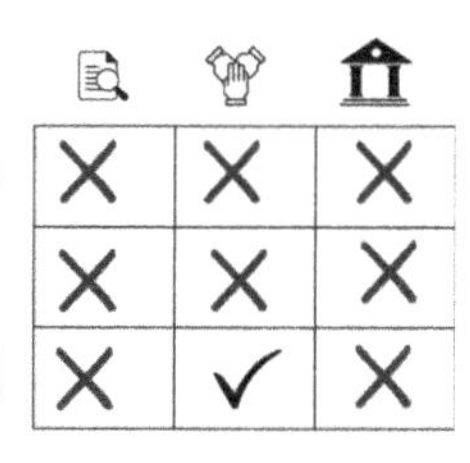

44.

The murderer is Temporal Tinkerer. The motive was linked to professional rivalry, and manipulating the time loop device was a way to eliminate Dr. Quasar Quirk and secure Temporal Tinkerer's position as the leading temporal scientist.

45.

The murderer is Victor Vector. The motive was linked to professional rivalry, and manipulating the cosmic codes was a way to eliminate Dr. Celestia Cipher and establish Victor Vector as the leading data analyst in astrophysics.

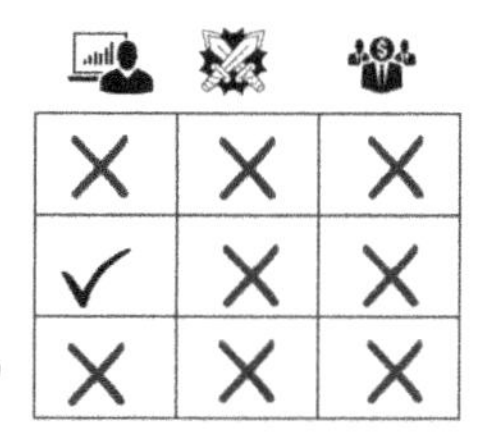

46.

The murderer is Theo Theoremquest. The motive was linked to professional rivalry, and tampering with the quantum experiment with a paradoxical twist was a way to eliminate Dr. Quark Quantumquest and establish Theo Theoremquest as the leading quantum theorist.

47.

The murderer is Cyber Cipher. The motive was linked to professional rivalry, and manipulating the digital code disrupting key systems was a way to eliminate Dr. Techno Tinkerer and assert control over the field of digital disruption.

48.

The murderer is Genome Guru. The motive was linked to ethical disagreements, and manipulating the gene-editing tool with altered DNA sequences was a way to eliminate Dr. Gene Genesis and assert control over the field of biotechnology.

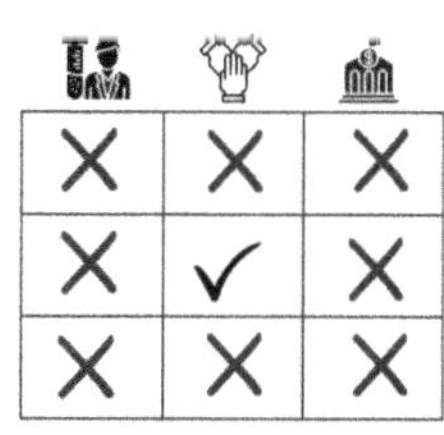

49.

The murderer is Victor Vortex. The motive was linked to unresolved scientific disputes, and tampering with the quantum experiment causing dimensional disarray was a way to eliminate Dr. Quasar Quandary and establish Victor Vortex as the leading quantum physicist.

	X	X	X
	X	X	X
	X	X	✓

50.

The murderer is Victor Virus. The motive was linked to professional rivalry, and manipulating the quantum hacking tool was a way to eliminate Dr. Firewalla and assert control over the field of quantum cybersecurity.

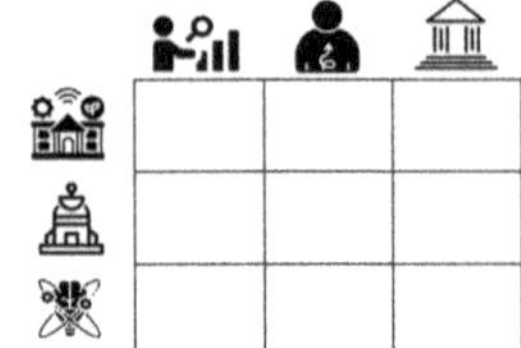